Fo

Forever I Am Changed
Copyright © 2011
One Man One Message
P.O. Box 8513
St. Louis, MO 63126
All Rights Reserved
onemanonemessage.org

Name: _____

Salvation Date: _____

Date Water Baptized: _____

Date Filled with the Holy Spirit: _____

Important Scriptures: _____

_____

_____

_____

Thoughts: _____

_____

_____

_____

_____

_____

_____

_____

_____

TABLE OF CONTENTS

FOREWORD

Every day of our lives brings change, whether we want it or not. There is something different about every day we live — the things we do and the things we don't do. As we encounter new experiences and new people, we inevitably go through change.

As you read through this booklet you will encounter new concepts which will invariably elicit some sort of change in you. Maybe significant, maybe subtle, but change nonetheless. You will experience a change of heart, a change of attitude, a change of how you look at yourself and how you look at the world. It won't be fleeting or momentary...it will be everlasting. You will be *forever changed*.

The purpose of this booklet is to share the life-changing message of salvation, and everything that comes with it, which is freely available to everyone who believes, thanks to One Man, Jesus. He is the Son of God who died on the cross so that whoever believes in Him shall have everlasting life.

Therefore, if anyone is in Christ, he is a new creation; old things have passed away; behold, all things have become new (**2 Corinthians 5:17** NKJV).

JESUS LOVES YOU

…He first loved us (**1 John 4:19** NKJV).

Jesus Loves You. *No matter what. Nothing* you could ever do or say — whatever your sins may be — could change the fact that Jesus loves you. You may not love Him or believe in Him. You may even hate Him. You may be angry with Him, or just not care about Him at all. None of that will ever change the fact that He loves you — He always has and He always will. There is *nothing — not one thing —* you can do to make Him stop loving you.

The world can be a tough place to live and you may feel like no one loves you or cares about you. You may feel like you are not worthy of being loved because of things you've done or because someone in your life has told you that you are not worthy of love. But the truth is no matter how you feel or why you feel the way you do, you can *always* cling to the fact that Jesus loves you and cares about you. He cares about all of us.

Jesus spent His entire ministry tending to the needs of other people. He healed the sick, the blind, the deaf, and the lame. He was a man of great compassion. He raised people from the dead. He forgave people of their sins. He fed the hungry and comforted the poor. He hung on the cross, dying for our sins. He asked God to forgive His accusers for they *knew not what they did*. His entire ministry was totally focused on caring for the needs of hurting people. (For specific references to all of these statements, read the **book of John in the Bible**).

The love of Jesus Christ is awesome. It is amazing. It is unlike anything you could ever imagine, **and it is yours**. No strings attached, at no cost to you. You don't have to buy it — you couldn't, even if you wanted to. It's not for sale. You don't have to do anything to earn it — you couldn't, no matter how hard you tried. You don't have to do anything for Jesus to love you. He just does. Not because of what we've done, ***but because that is who He is.*** Jesus *is* love. And **Jesus loves you!**

LOVE

So you must love one another (**John 13:34** NIV).

Love — a very simple word and a very complex emotion. There are books dedicated to this one topic alone, such as: finding love, falling in love, first love, staying in love, true love, unconditional love, falling out of love...all different kinds of love.

The focus of this section is not so much on the many definitions of love, but rather on the statement Jesus made in **John 13:34** (NIV) which is, *A new command I give you; Love one another. As I have loved you, so you must love one another*. Jesus makes it sound pretty simple — just love each other. Stop fighting with each other and just get along with one another.

Stop having petty disagreements, just set all of that stuff aside and love each other!

Loving one another is so important to God that He commands us to do so in **John 13:34** (NIV): *A new command I give you*. And again in **John 15:12** (NASB), Jesus says, *This is My commandment: that you love one another, just as I have loved you*. God does not say to love if you want to, or only love people who are nice to you or are lovable. He did not say, *"A new choice I give you."* No, He **commands** us to do so. He says we are to love one another as *He loves us.* That is a pretty high standard to measure up to — loving each other the same way Jesus loves us.

Ephesians 5:2 (AMP) says to *walk in love [esteeming and delighting in one another] as Christ loved us*. Jesus' love for us is so great that He gave His life for us on the cross. Think about that, seriously. Really think about that. He literally gave His life for us; He died so that we could live. For our salvation He died a brutal death on the cross. That is amazing, unconditional love. That is the great example we are to follow with respect to loving one another. **Colossians 3:14** (NKJV) goes as far as to say, *Above all these things put on love*. Meaning, literally make the choice every day to "put on" or wear love just as if it is part of our clothing. Walk in love with every step we take. Treat people with kindness and consideration, even when they may not deserve it or are not being lovable. Take the high road, turn the other check, or just let it go when someone treats us poorly.

Learning how to walk in love is a great way to grow in your relationship with the Lord. Praying **1 Corinthians 13:1-8** in The Amplified Bible every day is a great way to get started and keep walking in love. To make it more personal, insert "I" in the scripture as you read it out loud. [1]

There are certainly many other references in God's Word about love and of loving one another that you can read and meditate on as you focus on this area of your life. A few of these scriptures are provided below.

We love Him, because He first loved us (**1 John 4:19** AMP).

Dear friends, let us love one another, for love comes from God. Everyone who loves has been born of God and knows God. Whoever does not love does not know God, because God is love. This is how God showed his love among us: He sent his one and only Son into the world that we might live through him. This is love: not that we loved God, but that he loved us and sent his Son as an atoning sacrifice for our sins. Dear friends, since God so loved us, we also ought to love one another (**1 John 4:7-11** NIV).

By this all men will know that you are my disciples, if you love one another (**John 13:35** NIV).

Be devoted to one another in brotherly love. Honor one another above yourselves (**Romans 12:10** NIV).

[Love, for the Day is Near] Let no debt remain outstanding, except the continuing debt to love one another, for he who loves his fellowman has fulfilled the law (**Romans 13:8** NIV).

Be completely humble and gentle; be patient, bearing with one another in love (**Ephesians 4:2** NIV).

Now that you have purified yourselves by obeying the truth so that you have sincere love for your brothers, love one another deeply, from the heart (**1 Peter 1:22** NIV).

Greet one another with a kiss of love. Peace to all of you who are in Christ (**1 Peter 5:14** NIV).

[Love one another] This is the message you heard from the beginning: We should love one another (**1 John 3:11** NIV).

And this is his command: to believe in the name of his Son, Jesus Christ, and to love one another as he commanded us (**1 John 3:23** NIV).

Our prayer for you today, and every day you spend time with the Lord in His Word, is for you to gain an even greater understanding of how much He truly does love you — that you *feel* His amazing love for you!

LEARN

If you confess with your mouth that Jesus is Lord and believe in your heart that God raised him from the dead, you will be saved (**Romans 10:9** NLT).

Prayer of salvation, born again, saved, faith in Christ, giving your life to Christ, God's free gift, rebirth, new birth, new beginnings, new life, new lease on life... these are just some of the many phrases used to refer to that moment in time when you invite Jesus into your heart.

JESUS - WHOSOEVER BELIEVES IN HIM

This text will not get into a theological dissertation about Jesus (or God) or provide pages of explanation about why we believe what we believe. We simply believe in God and Jesus by faith.

We believe in the Bible. We believe there is one God who exists in three persons — God the Father, God the Son, and God the Holy Spirit. We believe that God is greater than anyone or anything in the world.

We believe Jesus Christ is our Lord and Savior, and He is the only begotten Son of the Father, conceived by the Holy Spirit, and born of the Virgin Mary. We believe He lived a life in the flesh, and because of this, He knows and understands our pain, weaknesses and temptations. We believe Jesus was crucified, died on the cross for our sins, was buried, and was raised from the dead on the third day. We believe He ascended into heaven and is seated at the right hand of the Father as our Intercessor. We believe that in order to go to God, we must go through Jesus, our Intercessor. It is through Jesus that we have a relationship with God the Father.

We believe that anyone who believes in God will have everlasting life with Him because **John 3:15** (NLT) says, *Everyone who believes in Me [Jesus] may have eternal life. We also believe, that if you confess with your mouth that Jesus is Lord and believe in your heart that God raised him from the dead, you will be saved. For it is by believing in your heart that you are made right with God, and it is by confessing with your mouth that you are saved. As the Scriptures tell us, Anyone who trusts in him will never be disgraced... for Everyone who calls on the name of the Lord will be saved* (**Romans 10:9-13** NLT). If you believe that too, or if you want to find out more, then you are in the right place. There is information in this booklet that can change your life forever, if you will only believe.

Our prayer for you: *Father God, we pray right now in the name of Jesus for every person reading this, that You would touch their lives in a special way. God, may they feel Your presence as they prepare to learn more about You and the awesome life you have in store for them. God, we pray that every word they read speaks to their heart and makes perfect sense, that nothing gets in the way of the message and what*

You would have them hear and understand. We thank You, God, for all that You are doing in each and every one of us. In Jesus' name we pray. Amen!

A PERSONAL RELATIONSHIP

Jesus loves you and wants to have a personal relationship with you — all you have to do is ask Him into your life and invite Him into your heart. No one can do it for you, and you can't do it for someone else. This is something deeply personal between you and the Lord. God gave His only Son, Jesus, to take away our sins and offer us a better life. Scripture says:

…I have come that they may have life, and that they may have it more abundantly (**John 10:10** NKJV).

For God so loved the world, that He gave His only begotten Son, that whosoever believeth in Him should not perish, but have everlasting life (**John 3:16** KJV).

All we have to do is invite Jesus into our heart. He is there waiting for us to simply ask. Jesus says in **Revelation 3:20** (NIV), *Here I am! I stand at the door and knock. If anyone hears my voice and opens the door, I will come in and eat with him, and he with me.*

ADMIT YOU ARE A SINNER - ASK FOR FORGIVENESS

Before inviting Jesus into our hearts, we must first admit that we have made mistakes and ask for His forgiveness. We are all sinners. We've all made mistakes. None of us are perfect. *For all have sinned, and come short of the glory of God* (**Romans 3:23** KJV). There is nothing at all to be ashamed of or embarrassed about doing this.

This is something between you and the Lord and no one else. You don't need to go to or through another person or leader in a church to get to Jesus — you can do this completely on your own. It is a matter of humbling yourself before the Lord and truly repenting for the wrong choices you've have made.

And don't think that you have done something so horrible that God won't forgive you. *Nothing* you have said or done is a surprise to God. He already knows it all. He knew what we would do before we were even born. He will forgive us. What is important is to come before the Lord remorsefully and sincerely, admitting you've made mistakes, saying you are sorry and asking for forgiveness. *Repent... that your sins may be wiped out, that and times of refreshing may come from the Lord* (**Acts 3:19** NIV).

BELIEVE THAT JESUS
DIED FOR YOUR SINS

Salvation is God's *free* gift to us. We did not do anything to earn salvation. We can't buy it anywhere. We need to simply believe that Jesus died on the cross to take away our sins. *...God showed His great love for us by sending His son Jesus to die for us while we were still sinners* (**Romans 5:8** NLT). Jesus paid the price for our sins by dying on the cross. He was the sacrificial lamb, shedding His blood and dying to reconcile us to God. He triumphed over the grave and is seated at the right hand of the Father as our Intercessor.

CONFESS THAT JESUS IS
LORD OF YOUR LIFE

Confessing that Jesus is the Lord of your life means letting go of your ways and the ways of the world and surrendering everything you are and everything you have to Him. No, that does not mean you need to sell everything you have or give away everything you own. Again, this is a matter of your heart. It means you are willing to give your life, your heart, to Jesus. It's an understanding that whatever the Lord has blessed you with belongs to Him; you are simply a caretaker of it. It means everything we do with our lives, we do for Jesus. He is our Lord and we have no other gods before Him. *I am the Lord Your God...you shall have no other gods before Me* (**Exodus 20:2-3** NIV).

PRAYER OF SALVATION

Are you ready to let go of your own ways and the
ways of the world to become a "new creation" in
Christ? This is not just about saying some words
as part of a prayer. This is about truly believing in
your heart that Jesus died for you, that He is your
Lord and Savior, and you are ready to let go of your
past, confess your sins, and give up your "old" way
of living life in the world and start living your life
for Jesus. If you are ready to do all of that, then you
are ready to pray the prayer of salvation. ***This will
be the most important prayer you ever say. Speak
the following words out loud to the Lord with a
completely sincere heart.***

*Lord Jesus, I admit that I am a sinner. I ask You to
forgive me, Lord, and cleanse me of my sins. I believe
You are the Son of the Most High God. I believe
You died on the cross and shed Your blood for me. I
confess You are the Lord of my life and I surrender
my life to You. You are my Savior, my Lord, my God.
Come into my heart. Change me forever. In Jesus'
name I pray. Amen!*

Welcome to the kingdom of God! If you just prayed
this prayer and accepted Jesus into your heart, His
Word says you are born again. *If you confess with
your mouth that Jesus is Lord and believe in your
heart that God raised him from the dead, you will
be saved. For it is by believing in your heart that
you are made right with God, and it is by confessing*

with your mouth that you are saved (**Romans 10:9-10** NLT). *For whosoever shall call upon the name of the Lord shall be saved* (**Romans 10:13** KJV). You are "whosoever" and you are now saved! **Congratulations! We joyfully celebrate with you!**

GROW – LIFE AFTER SALVATION

…If any of you wants to be my follower, you must turn from your selfish ways, take up your cross, and follow Me… (**Mark 8:34** NLT).

Now what? You just prayed the prayer of salvation and gave your life to Jesus, and you may be asking, *What do I do now?* It can certainly be overwhelming trying to figure out what to do next. The good news is that there aren't any formulas, checklists, rules or regulations to follow, but there are some things you will need to know to help get you started in the right direction.

The following pages contain a lot of great information to help you develop and grow in your personal relationship with Jesus. Your relationship with the Lord is very similar to other relationships you have in your life in that you need to spend time nurturing and developing it. You should spend as much time with Him as you can on a daily basis, praying, reading the Bible, going to a good Bible-based church, listening to teachings and music inspired by the Holy Spirit, and so much more. These areas will be covered in greater detail throughout this booklet.

Are you ready to get to know Jesus even better? If so, let's get started!

BECOMING A NEW
CREATURE IN CHRIST

Therefore if any man be in Christ, he is a new creature: old things are passed away; behold, all things are become new (**2 Corinthians 5:17** KJV).

Becoming a new creature in Christ....What does that mean? When you prayed the prayer of salvation and gave your life to Christ, you became a new person. **2 Corinthians 5:17** (TLB) says, *When someone becomes a Christian, he becomes a brand new person inside. He is not the same anymore. A new life has begun!*

So, what is new? Is it your appearance? Not really. You probably look the same physically. But you may **feel** a little different. Maybe a little more peaceful, like a burden has been lifted. Now that you are "in Christ," your sins are forgiven and forgotten and your past life is history — nothing you did will be held against you. You have a new beginning. God is not keeping an account of your former sins, nor should you. It's time to let go of your past mistakes — those days are now over, passed away. You may start looking at life and the world a little differently than you used to, make different choices, and have a better perspective of things.

Our salvation is one of the most important aspects of our lives. But if we stopped there, we would not experience the complete victory Jesus died for us to have. A big part of this victory is in how we live our lives each and every day **after** our salvation in preparation for how we will spend our lives for eternity.

Mark 8:34-35 (NLT) says, *...If any of you wants to be my follower, you must turn from your selfish ways, take up your cross, and follow me. If you try to hang on to your life, you will lose it. But if you give up your life for my sake and for the sake of the Good News, you will save it*. You may be wondering what living a new life for Jesus is all about. The Grow section of the booklet has information that can help you find out.

Our prayer for you: *"Father, we pray for every person reading this that the information presented in the* **Grow** *section of this booklet will help them start the next step of their journey with You. We pray their hearts are receptive and the Holy Spirit gives then supernatural understanding of everything they read in the* **Grow** *section. We pray they are blessed and continue to be touched by You as they learn and grow in Your presence. We pray this in the name of Jesus. Amen!"* Let's get growing!

THE BIBLE

For the Word of God is living and active. Sharper than any double-edged sword... (**Hebrews 4:12** NIV).

The Bible, God's Word, The Word of God, The Good Book, The Living Word...these are just a few names used to refer to the Bible.

Whatever you prefer to use when referring to the Bible, the most important thing is that you have a Bible and you read it often! (Note: For the purposes of this booklet, we are not going to provide a history or theological assessment of the Bible. There are many other resources which provide wonderful explanations about the Bible and its history. There are also books you can research if you want to find an in-depth study about the history and origin of the Bible). Simply put, we believe the Bible is the literal, infallible and complete Word of God. We believe it was written by people inspired by the Holy Spirit. We believe the events documented in the Bible actually happened and are historically correct and factual. The Bible is the one authority on which we base our lives. We believe the more time we spend reading God's Word, the better our relationship is with Him. So, with that in mind, we begin with the importance of using the Bible to develop a personal relationship with the Lord.

DEVELOPING A
PERSONAL RELATIONSHIP

The depth of our relationship with the Lord is directly related to the depth of our relationship with His Word, the Bible. The Bible is God's Word; it is God talking directly to us. When we read it, we should read it from the perspective of God sharing His thoughts and ways with us. We need to set aside any preconceived notions or opinions about what we think about life and our life situations and look to the Word of God to see what He has to say. He is the ultimate authority — we should always defer to His Word. We should never let our own opinions or experiences, or those of other people, interpret the Word of God for us. Rather, we should allow His Word to speak for itself and establish the truth.

At the same time, when we read the Word, we need to make sure we are hearing what **God** is saying in His Word and not twist or filter it to accommodate our own desires. We also need to be careful not to form opinions on what we believe based on someone else's preconceived notions of who God is. We need to make sure our beliefs are scripturally sound.

Paul tells us in **1 Thessalonians 2:13** (AMP) ...*When you received the message of God [which you heard] from us, you welcomed it not as the word of [mere] men, but as it truly is, the Word of God, which is effectually at work in you who believe [exercising its superhuman power in those who adhere to and trust* *in and rely on it].* When we truly hear and understand the Word of God — with our hearts and not just with our heads — there is "superhuman power" available to us as we **adhere to and trust in and rely on it**. That is an awesome Word from God! If we let Him speak to us through His Word, then we will have superhuman power available to us as believers!

Because of this promise from the Lord, we should always be careful not to deceive ourselves or others through the misinterpretation of God's Word. Job addressed this in **Job 42:1-6** (MSG) when he says, *I'm convinced: You can do anything and everything. Nothing and no one can upset Your plans. You asked, 'who is this muddying the water, ignorantly confusing the issue, second-guessing My purposes?' I admit it. I was the one. I babbled on about things far beyond me, made small talk about wonders way over my head. You told me, 'Listen, and let Me do the talking. Let Me ask the questions. You give the answers.' **I admit I once lived by rumors of you; now I have it all firsthand—from my own eyes and ears!** I'm sorry—forgive me. I'll never do that again, I promise! I'll never again live on crusts of hearsay, crumbs of rumor.*

Every time we get ready to spend time in the Word with the Lord, we need to ask God to cleanse our hearts and minds of any misconceptions or preconceived notions about what we think we know or others may have told us, and we need to ask Him to show us exactly what He wants us to see and hear. If we do this, the Word of God will certainly be

...a lamp to my feet and a light to my path (**Psalm 119:105** NKJV). The Word of God is a road map for our lives. Everything we experience in our lives, everything we are going through, any question we have, can be found and addressed in the Word of God.

HOW DO I GET STARTED?

For those of us who did not grow up having a Bible, much less reading one or being taught how to read one, the questions of **how** and **where** to get started are very good ones.

First step, get a Bible. As you may know there are several (okay, more like **many**) different versions of the Bible. Which one is best for you? There really is not a right or wrong answer; it is more a matter of your personal preference. If someone tries to tell you a particular version is *the* only right one or another version is not the right one, they are being "religious" and it would be better for you to respectfully disregard those opinions. God's Word is God's Word.

Different versions allow God to speak to different kinds of people in many different ways. For example, a passage in The Amplified Bible (AMP) may make more sense to one person than it does to another. That same passage may make more sense in the King James Version (KJV) to someone else. The point is, we should read the Bible. The more we read the Bible the more we'll we understand it, and the more

we will be able to grow in our relationship with the
Lord. Some people may have multiple versions of the
Bible. Depending on the passage, it may make more
sense to them in one version than it does in another.
Yet, there may be one version you prefer more than
all the others.

If you don't have a Bible, or if you have one and
want to get a different version, check your area for a
Christian bookstore. They should have a wide variety
of Bibles to choose from. Or, you can go online and
do a search for Bible retail stores. Most locations
should have a very large selection of Bibles to choose
from and will also likely offer specialty versions for
men, women, kids, teens, etc. Take a look at **Genesis
3:8** (below) to get an idea of the differences in some
of the versions of the Bible.

Genesis 3:8

King James Version (KJV)
*And they heard the voice of the LORD God walking
in the garden in the cool of the day: and Adam and
his wife hid themselves from the presence of the
LORD God amongst the trees of the garden.*

New King James Version (NKJV)
*And they heard the sound of the LORD God walking
in the garden in the cool of the day, and Adam and
his wife hid themselves from the presence of the
LORD God among the trees of the garden.*

New International Version (NIV)
Then the man and his wife heard the sound of the LORD God as he was walking in the garden in the cool of the day, and they hid from the LORD God among the trees of the garden.

New American Standard (NAS)
They heard the sound of the LORD God walking in the garden in the cool of the day, and the man and his wife hid themselves from the presence of the LORD God among the trees of the garden.

The Message Bible (MSG)
When they heard the sound of GOD strolling in the garden in the evening breeze, the Man and his Wife hid in the trees of the garden, hid from GOD.

The Amplified Version (AMP)
And they heard the sound of the Lord God walking in the garden in the cool of the day, and Adam and his wife hid themselves from the presence of the Lord God among the trees of the garden.

New Living Translation (NLT)
When the cool evening breezes were blowing, the man and his wife heard the LORD God walking about in the garden. So they hid from the LORD God among the trees.

If you have never read the Bible before, you may want to consider buying a Daily Devotional Bible or a Bible organized by topic. These type of Bibles typically give you a good starting point and some supporting explanations of the scriptures you are reading. These Bibles can take you on a great journey through the Word on a daily basis or based on a specific area you feel you need to focus on. You can also consider starting with the book of **John** or **Psalms.** These are also good starting points to get into the Word.

There are also three scriptures from the Amplified Bible we encourage you pray on a daily basis to help build your relationship with the Lord: **1 Corinthians 13:1-8**[1], **Ephesians 3:14-20**[2] and **Colossians 1:9-14**[3]. These scriptures have been modified in this booklet by inserting "I" to personalize them to be read from your perspective. When prayed on a daily basis over several months, the messages from these scriptures will indwell your spirit and you will experience a wonderful transformation in your heart for the Lord and for others.

As you continue spending time in the Word on a daily basis, your Bible will begin to feel like a good friend. When you spend time in the Word, reading what God has to say to His people — to you — you will find great comfort, peace, joy, happiness, love and so much more. Your Bible can get you through some difficult times. When you are facing a difficult situation and you pick up your Bible, you can immediately feel a sense of comfort because you know God's Word is personal and powerful and waiting for you! *He will meet you right where you are, whatever you are going through, whenever you pick up His Word.*

READING THE BIBLE

Don't ever be afraid, ashamed or embarrassed to read the Bible. Don't ever think that you are not smart enough or educated enough or a good enough person to read the Bible. There is tremendous power available to you in God's Word.

The Bible is food for your spirit. Just like we eat food throughout the day, every day, to feed our physical bodies, we need to stay in the Word to feed our spirit — to keep it growing. We can't just go to church on Sunday and hear a message and think it will maintain us for the entire week. We wouldn't just eat a meal on Sunday morning and then eat nothing else the rest of the week, would we? We usually eat three meals a day, with snacks in between, to maintain our physical bodies. The same should be true for our spiritual well-being. We should feed ourselves daily on the Word of God. We should be doers of the Word, putting the Word to work in our lives, exercising our spiritual muscles so we can grow and develop in the Word of God.

Carve out some time each day to read the Word. If you are just getting started, that may be as little as 5 minutes at the beginning of every day. It should be a time you set aside just for you and the Lord to spend together. No TV, no radio, no phones, no computers or other distractions — just you, your Bible and the Lord. Ask anyone living with you not to interrupt you, to respect the time you are spending with the Lord. He is our first priority. When we give Him the first part of our day, He will help to prepare us for the day ahead. No matter what distractions or issues come up when you start reading the Word do your best to keep your focus to spend that time with the Lord in His Word!

Just a quick note: The freedom to read the Bible is an incredible blessing and privilege that should never be taken for granted. There are, however, some countries in the world whose citizens are not allowed to read or own a Bible. In fact, they may persecute people who own, read or try to give away Bibles. If you are among those who are freely able to read your Bible on a daily basis, make it a habit to pray for fellow Christians who are persecuted for wanting to read the Word of God. Pray they will be allowed to have the same freedoms you experience to read the Word and develop a relationship with the Lord without fear of persecution.

BIBLE STUDY

Consider joining a Bible study. Many churches offer this as a resource to help people get into the Word and learn more. It's a great way to get involved with others who also have a passion for God's Word. Be sure whoever is teaching the Bible study is teaching strictly from the Word. If you find that they are offering more of their own opinions than what the Bible itself says, try to find another group with an instructor who is teaching strictly from the Bible.

There are also many resources you can buy and work through on your own to study the Bible. These resources are good because they allow you to focus on areas of interest to you and you can work at your own pace. One such tool you may find useful for your Bible study time is a concordance. A concordance is a dictionary of words that provides listings of scriptures related to those words. For example, if you want to know every reference and use of the word *love* in the Bible, you would look up the word *love* in a concordance and it would list all the scriptures where love is referenced. This could be useful to you if there is a specific area in your life you want to research in the Bible.

There are many different types of concordances as well. You can check your local Christian bookstore or search online. And just like the versions of the Bible, there is no right or wrong concordance; it is a matter of personal preference and what works best for you.

Our prayer for you today and every day is regardless of *how* you decide to study the Word that you make it a point to do it every day. There is power, understanding and peace in the Word of God we pray becomes available to you as you spend time in the Word. We pray God shows you everything He wants you to see and know every time you pick up your Bible and spend time with Him in His Word.

PRAYER

Pray continually (**1 Thessalonians 5:17** NIV). There are a lot of different words and ways people use to describe talking to God; praying or prayer tend to be the most common. Then there are the questions of how to pray, when to pray, where to pray, what to say, how to start, how long to pray, how to end.... Before we know it, we can get so caught up in what we think we are supposed to do, we lose track of what we were doing in the first place — talking to God.

HOW TO PRAY

There is no formula for prayer, such as start this way, end this way, say these things, spend this much time, bow your head, fold your hands, get down on your knees.... Like most everything else we've already presented, prayer is a matter of your heart, or your attitude, before the Lord. You can pray anytime, anywhere, any way, for any reason. You don't have to bow your head or fold your hands, but you can if you want to, if that is what you are comfortable with. God doesn't care if you are sitting, standing or kneeling. It is about spending time with Him and believing in your heart that He hears your prayers and will answer them.

Let's camp on the "believing He will answer your prayers" part for a minute. Does that mean if we believe God, He will answer our prayers for millions of dollars, nice cars, beautiful homes and many other material goods? It's hard to say. Maybe, if that's His will for your life. But consider this: Do you give your children everything they ask for? "Mommy, Daddy, can I have this toy, that game, money for candy, money for ice cream," or whatever childish demand they come to you with? Hopefully not, because that could create a very difficult, spoiled and unappreciative child. Hopefully, as a parent you carefully evaluate and consider every request made by your children and determine what is in their best interest to provide for them. God is the same way with us. We don't need to go to God in prayer whining and complaining and begging "Please, please, please, please, God, give me a nice house." Just like we would not want our kids asking us "Please, please, please, please give me a new bike and I will never ask for anything again, and I will leave you alone. I promise — pleeeeeaaaasssseeeee..." Right — until the next time!

Just like we use wisdom with our own children and don't give them every single thing they ask for, we need to trust God and believe that He knows exactly what we, His children, need when we need it, and how to answer every single one of our prayers. He tells us in **1 John 5:14** (AMP), *And this is the confidence (the assurance, the privilege of boldness) which we have in Him: [we are sure] that if we ask anything (make any request) according to His will (in agreement with His own plan), He listens to and hears us.* So, we need to do our part, pray, and trust God to do His part. That means not questioning why or when God will answer our prayers, but truly trusting we have done our part in prayer, letting God be God, and trusting Him to take care of the rest. There may be times when it *looks* like nothing is happening or our prayers are not being answered, but we can't stop trusting God. He is always working behind the scenes on our behalf. It may not be how we would take care of the situation, but we have to trust and believe God has every circumstance and situation under control. He is God — there is not one thing He cannot do.

Be anxious for nothing, but in everything by prayer and supplication with thanksgiving let your requests be made known to God. And the peace of God, which surpasses all comprehension, will guard your hearts and your minds in Christ Jesus (**Philippians 4:6-7** NASB).

Praying to God should be as simple as talking to your best friend, actually easier. Even best friends are sometimes hard to talk to. It should never be hard to talk to God. There's nothing you can't say to Him. **Nothing! Philippians 4:6** (AMP) says, *Do not fret or have any anxiety about anything, but in every circumstance and in everything, by prayer and petition (definite requests), with thanksgiving, continue to make your wants known to God.* He will never judge what you have to say. He will never laugh at you. He will never make fun of you. He will never use what you say against you later on. He will never tell anyone else what you tell Him. He will ALWAYS listen to you. He ALWAYS cares. He will ALWAYS be there for you any time of the day or night. You can pray about anything and everything. Nothing is so big that God cannot handle it. Nothing is so small that God does not care about it. *Give all your worries and cares to God, for he cares about you* (**1 Peter 5:7** NLT).

HOW OFTEN SHOULD WE PRAY?

When and how often should we pray? **Romans 12:12** (NIV) says, *Be joyful in hope, patient in affliction, faithful in prayer and* **1 Thessalonians 5:17** (NASB) says to *pray without ceasing.* Does that mean literally every minute of the day? No. Again, it's more about having a heart that is sensitive to the Lord as you go about your day. Prayer is about creating a relationship with the Lord, spending time with Him, becoming familiar with Him, creating or making time during each day to talk to the Lord. Don't pray only when you have problems or need help. Talk to the Lord as much as you can throughout the day and make it part of your everyday life. For example, when you wake up in the morning, try to keep your first thoughts and the first words out of your mouth focused on the Lord. Resist thoughts like, "Oh, I am so tired. Ugh, I don't want to go to work…school…or get up and take care of the kids." Instead, strive to begin your day with thoughts like, "Thank You, God, for this day. *This is the day the LORD has made; let us rejoice and be glad in it* (**Psalm 118:24** NASB).

Thank God for good health, the breath of life, and whatever else you are thankful for that day. Continue to dialogue with Him all day long, sharing what is in your heart and on your mind. Pray over and thank Him for every meal you have during the day. Thank Him for the great day you're having, for family and friends in your life, for the sunrise, flowers, trees, life's simplest pleasures. Be thankful for running water, electricity, everything you have that is a

blessing to you. Pray at the end of the day and thank
the Lord for the day, His protection and your safety.
Pray for blessings for your friends and family, as
well as anything and everything else you can think
of praying about. Create a lifestyle where prayer and
thanking the Lord is always on your mind and being
expressed out of your mouth. Make it a point to set
aside some time when all you do is spend time with
the Lord in prayer.

As you go through every day, try taking everything
that comes your way in life to God in prayer before
you talk with anyone else about it. The next time
"life happens" and your first inclination is to talk
to a friend and get their opinion, try going to God
first and talking to Him about any problems, issues,
concerns, or needs you may have. Consider saying,
"God, I can't handle this situation; it's too big for me.
I need Your help. I give this situation to You and ask
for Your help. Show me what You would have me do
and show me how I can get out of the way so You can
take care of the rest."

It seems so often we try to handle everything
ourselves, to solve problems with our own strength
or ask friends for their opinions to figure things out.
But instead of spending all of that time analyzing a
problem, we can give the cares of this life to God
and let Him take care of them. **2 Corinthians 12:9**
(AMP) says His strength is enough to overcome
our weaknesses. In addition, **1 Peter 5:7** (NLT)
says, *Give all your worries and cares to God, for he*

cares about you. And Paul tells us in **Philippians 4:6** (AMP), *Do not fret or have any anxiety about anything, but in every circumstance and in everything, by prayer and petition, with thanksgiving, continue to make your wants known to God.* Casting our cares upon the Lord is a great way to free up our minds and hearts for the more joyful things in life.

NEVER BE AFRAID TO PRAY

Praying out loud, or just praying at all, may be something new to you or something that you are not completely comfortable with doing yet, and that is okay. *Never* be afraid or embarrassed or ashamed to pray. Just like anything else you learn for the first time, you will become more comfortable with it the more you do it. And in this case, the more you pray and read the Bible, the more you'll learn. Always know you can talk to God at any time, for any reason. God will listen to the prayer of a three-year-old child just as closely and with just as much love and concern as He would listen to the prayer of someone who has been praying for eighty years. So no matter where you are in your relationship with the Lord, always know He is there for you at all times.

If someone asks you to pray with them and you are not comfortable doing so, that's okay. Just be honest with them. Let them know you are not comfortable praying out loud with them at that exact moment, but you would be happy to cover a particular issue in prayer for them when you are alone with the

Lord. As you spend more time in prayer and develop your relationship with God, you will also develop confidence and boldness praying for others. **Just take it all one step and one day at a time.**

Lastly, there is no need to ever compare your prayer life or how you pray to how someone else prays or what they sound like when they pray. Our prayer life is personal to each of us and is between us and God, not us and other people. Don't pray to be seen or heard by other people — prayer is about spending time with God. So be sure when you pray that you are mindful of what is said in **Matthew 6:5-8** (NIV):

Also when you pray, you must not be like the hypocrites, for they love to pray standing in the synagogues and on the corners of the streets, that they may be seen by people. Truly I tell you, they have their reward in full already. But when you pray, go into your [most] private room, and, closing the door, pray to your Father, Who is in secret; and your Father, Who sees in secret, will reward you in the open. And when you pray, do not heap up phrases (multiply words, repeating the same ones over and over) as the Gentiles do, for they think they will be heard for their much speaking. Do not be like them, for your Father knows what you need before you ask Him.

GOD ANSWERS PRAYER

God really does answer prayer. It may not *look* like it to you right now. It may not *feel* like it to you right now. It may not be when or how you want it to be. It may not be the way we expect it or exactly what we are looking for. But God does answer prayer.

We need to get our thoughts and plans out of our heads and yield to Him, His timing and His answers. His ways, thoughts and plans are so much greater than our ways, thoughts and plans. God tell us in **Isaiah 55:9** (AMP), *For as the heavens are higher than the earth, so are My ways higher than your ways and My thoughts than your thoughts*. Believe, by faith, that God hears your prayers and answers them. **Second Corinthians 5:7** (NIV) says, *We live by faith, not by sight*. Meaning, we cannot be moved by what we see in the world, what we see in our everyday lives. We need to look away from all of that and believe in our hearts our prayers are working and God is taking care of our needs. Don't focus on what your circumstances may look like, but keep believing and praying, for *Jesus told His disciples…that they should always pray and not give up* (**Luke 18:1** NIV).

PRAYER REQUEST

There are many ministries and churches all over the world you can contact with a prayer request, including *OneManOneMessage.org/prayerrequest*. They will pray over your request and stand in agreement with you for your need to be met. So, whenever you have a prayer need, be sure to tap into these great resources available to you.

But also remember you still need to do your part too. *You* still need to keep praying about your needs. Don't just send in a prayer request and let someone else pray over your situation. If you can, ask a friend to pray with you and for you. The Bible says, *For where two or three come together in my name, there am I with them* (**Matthew 18:20** NIV). When you pray in agreement with someone else, God is right there with you. But be sure to let God hear *your* voice and *your* prayers as well.

WORD TEACHINGS/TEACHERS

For I give you sound teaching; Do not abandon my instruction (**Proverbs 4:2** NASB).

A great way to grow in your relationship with the Lord is to find resources, such as books, CDs or DVDs with teachings by anointed pastors and church leaders. The Lord has raised up great pastors and leaders in the body of Christ who have shared their experiences and practical life applications of God's Word in their everyday lives. The resources created through these pastors/teachers can be a great source of information, comfort, learning, or growing for whatever needs you have in life. The key to these teachings is they are created by people who have a true love for the Lord and a heart to help hurting people. They are doctrinally sound — they are based on the Word of God, and they are practical and can be applied to most situations you are going through.

To help get you started, a short listing is provided with some of the men and women God has used to teach His Word and share their tests and triumphs at *onemanonemessage.org/resources*. You may find exactly what you need in a particular area or you may find a particular individual's teaching or preaching style just doesn't work for you. That's okay. Everyone has their own style and each of us has our own preferences. That is why there are several references to choose from. If you can't get what you need from one person, chances are you can find it from someone else. Each individual perspective is very unique, but they all have one thing in common — *their unconditional love for the Lord, His Word, and a desire to help others who are going through circumstances and difficulties they too have experienced.*

This list is by no means exhaustive. There are many other pastors who have great teachings from the Lord. You may be blessed to have a pastor with anointed teachings in your local church. But regardless of *who* is providing the message, it's very important the message be based on the Word of God and it ministers to you in whatever situation you are going through. It is also important to mention these resources are meant to be a *supplement*, not a *replacement*, to spending time in God's Word. Books and teaching CDs can certainly help to explain, teach, enlighten, and enhance the messages in God's Word.

The time you spend reading books and listening to anointed teachings will absolutely help you to grow in your relationship with the Lord, but nothing should ever take the place of reading the Bible on your own and hearing what God has to say directly to you.

It is also probably worth mentioning when spending time reading, watching or listening to teachings, we should never make that message or teaching about the pastor or the person delivering the message. In other words, we should never make more of the pastor/ teacher than the Lord. Pastors/teachers are people just like we are. We all have our own gifts given to us by the Lord. Their gift is to share the Word of God, but the focus is the Lord, not the messenger. We are nothing without Him and everything with Him. And that applies to pastors/preachers/teachers the same way it applies to each one of us. Never put a pastor/preacher/teacher on a pedestal because of their teachings or a word God gave to them. These people are vessels God is using to share His Word — nothing more, nothing less.

Our prayer as you learn more about the Lord and the people He's called to share His Word, that you find the right book, CD, or DVD with the perfect message for the need you find yourself facing today. We pray God's Word will minister to you through the many testimonies and teachings which are available to you because we know what God has done for another He can also do for you. Peter tells us in **Acts 10:34** (AMP), ...*I now perceive and understand that God shows no partiality and is no respecter of persons.* What God has done for one person, He can most certainly do for you as well. In Jesus' name we pray that you find the perfect anointed message to meet you right where you are.

PRAISE AND WORSHIP

Let everything that has breath praise the LORD (**Psalm 150:6** NIV).

Praise means to "applaud, honor, glorify, admire." There are many different ways we can praise other people, such as saying nice things about them, telling them how much they mean to us, etc. But when it comes to praising the Lord, it's almost as if the word praise takes on a whole new meaning. It's like trying to find the right words to say thank you to someone who has literally saved your life, because that is what God has done for each and every one of us — He has given us new life in Him. How can we adequately thank Him for everything He has done for us? What can we do or say to the one we love most to show our appreciation for everything He has done? If we look to His Word (as we should on all occasions), it tells us the various ways we can honor God for all the things He has done for us.

Make a joyful noise unto the Lord.

Below are just a few of the really wonderful scriptures about praising and worshiping God.

Psalm 33:3 (NIV)
Sing to him a new song; play skillfully, and shout for joy.

Psalm 95:1-2 (NIV)
Come, let us sing for joy to the LORD; let us shout aloud to the Rock of our salvation. Let us come before him with thanksgiving and extol him with music and song.

Psalm 98:4 (NIV)
Shout for joy to the LORD, all the earth, burst into jubilant song with music.

Psalm 150:1-5 (NIV)
Praise the LORD. Praise God in his sanctuary; praise him in his mighty heavens. Praise him for his acts of power; praise him for his surpassing greatness. Praise him with the sounding of the trumpet, praise him with the harp and lyre, praise him with tambourine and dancing, praise him with the strings and flute, praise him with the clash of cymbals, praise him with resounding cymbals.

Psalm 146:2 (NIV)
I will praise the LORD all my life; I will sing praise to my God as long as I live.

Hebrews 13:15 (AMP)
…Let us constantly and at all times offer up to God a sacrifice of praise….

Psalm 47:1 (NLT)
…Shout to God with joyful praise!

Philippians 4:4 (KJV)
Rejoice in the Lord always: and again I say, Rejoice.

Psalm 134:2 (NIV)
*Lift up your hands in the sanctuary and praise the
LORD.*

Psalm 46:10 (NIV)
*Be still and know that I am God; I will be exalted
among the nations, I will be exalted in the earth.*

Listening to anointed praise and worship music is a
really great way to spend time in the presence of the
Lord. Just like there are many God-inspired teachers
of the Word, God has also raised up some tremendous
"ministers of music" in the body of Christ as well.
If you have never listened to praise and worship
music before, then you are in for a very pleasant and
enjoyable experience. If you already listen, then you
know what a blessing anointed praise and worship
music can be.

Spending time with the Lord while listening to praise
and worship music is an awesome way to grow in
your relationship with Him. You can always play
it around the house or in the car, or you can block
out a special time to spend with the Lord while
listening to worship music. If you are making time
to be alone with God, block out all other distractions
around you. Just like when you spend time with the
Lord in the Word, this is time for just you and Him,
with no interruptions, no phones, no computers or

anyone else. It's time you set aside — to get into His presence through music. Sing along if you want to; it will enhance your time with the Lord. It doesn't matter if you can sing well or not. Never be afraid or embarrassed to "make a joyful noise unto the Lord," regardless of what anyone else might say or think. God will love it, and that is all that matters.

If you are not familiar with praise and worship music and have never listened to it before, visit *onemanonemessage.org/resources* for a few suggestions. The type or style of worship music you enjoy and can relate to is a matter of personal preference. As long as the music is praising and glorifying God and bringing your relationship with Him to a higher level, then **it is the right music for *you***.

CHURCH

...Observe the Sabbath day by keeping it holy... **(Deuteronomy 5:12** NLT**)**.

Why should you go to church? Why is church important? Why not just stay home and read the Bible and listen to praise and worship music and God-inspired teachings and pray on your own? Sure, doing these things will most certainly help you grow in your relationship with the Lord. Once you've accepted Jesus as your Lord and Savior, in addition to reading the Bible and learning the Word, setting aside time each week to spend with God in church is another great way to grow in your relationship with Him. It is a great place to learn about the Word of God and develop your personal relationship with the Lord by getting in His presence. It is also a good place to meet other born-again believers and develop friendships with other godly people.

Hebrews 10:25 (NIV) says, *Let us not give up meeting together, as some are in the habit of doing, but let us encourage one another.* People can be deceived into thinking they don't need to go to church. For some, going to church is more of a chore and a hassle than a choice. Don't view going to church as something you **have** to do; view it as another effective way to spend time with the Lord and receiving the Word of God so you can be encouraged and encourage others.

If you are looking for a new church to go to but don't know where to get started, pray. Ask the Lord to show you where He would have you go. Ask friends and coworkers if they have any recommendations. Plan to visit some churches, attend services, meet some of the people in the church, and see if the services are something that you enjoy and will help you grow in the Lord. You will know when you find the right church for you.

GIVING/TITHING

...On the first [day] of each week, let each one of you [personally] put aside something and save it up as he has prospered [in proportion to what he is given]... (**1 Corinthians 16:2** AMP).

What is a tithe? Tithing is defined as "the tenth part of agricultural produce or personal income set apart as an offering to God or for works of mercy." It is giving the Lord the first fruits of your labors, the first ten percent of anything you produce. Typically, this is based on the gross income you receive. **First Corinthians 16:2** (AMP) says, *On the first [day] of each week, let each one of you [personally] put aside something and save it up as he has prospered [in proportion to what he is given]....*

People tend to have a lot of different opinions about tithing, such as: what it means, how much to give, how often and who to give to. This booklet will not provide a theological discussion about tithing. Very simply, we believe in tithing. We believe that *everything* we have belongs to the Lord: our homes, clothes, vehicles, money, every material possession as well as our personal relationships, belong to the Lord. We are merely stewards of the things He blesses us with. Our role is to take care of them and make good decisions about them. We believe in giving God our "first fruits" — the first ten percent of everything He blesses us with. Scripture says:

...Will a man rob God? Yet you rob me. But you ask, How do we rob you? In tithes and offerings. You are under a curse—the whole nation of you—because you are robbing me. Bring the whole tithe into the storehouse, that there may be food in my house. Test me in this, says the LORD Almighty, and see if I will not throw open the floodgates of heaven and pour out so much blessing that you will not have room enough for it. I will prevent pests from devouring your crops, and the vines in your fields will not cast their fruit, says the LORD Almighty. Then all the nations will call you blessed, for yours will be a delightful land, says the LORD Almighty (**Malachi 3:8-12** NIV).*

No, God does not **need** our money. He's God. Every resource in the world belongs to Him. He made it. He owns it. Tithing is much more about our hearts than it is about our bank accounts. It is about a spirit of giving, giving joyfully to the Lord and not out of a spirit of obligation. **Second Corinthians 9:7** (NLT) says, *You must each decide in your heart how much to give. And don't give reluctantly or in response to pressure, for God loves a person who gives cheerfully.* God is looking for us to be cheerful givers.

How you want to approach tithing and giving above and beyond your tithes is between you and the Lord. We encourage you to read what He says about it in scripture and go to Him in prayer and make a decision on tithing for yourself/your family. As it has been with all of the information we have presented to you, it is your decision to make. Your relationship with the Lord is exclusively yours and no one else's. How you want to approach that in the area of tithing is totally up to you and no one else. You shouldn't decide it for someone else and no one else should decide it for you.

Consider **Luke 16:9-13** (NLT), *Here's the lesson: Use your worldly resources to benefit others and make friends. Then, when your earthly possessions are gone, they will welcome you to an eternal home. If you are faithful in little things, you will be faithful in large ones. But if you are dishonest in little things, you won't be honest with greater responsibilities. And if you are untrustworthy about worldly wealth, who will trust you with the true riches of heaven? And if you are not faithful with other people's things, why should you be trusted with things of your own? No one can serve two masters. For you will hate one and love the other; you will be devoted to one and despise the other. You cannot serve both God and money.*

BAPTISM IN WATER

...what are you waiting for? Get up, be baptized and wash your sins away... (**Acts 22:16** NIV).

Water Baptism, baptism by water, baptism of Jesus, cleansing of sins, new beginning, these are just a few of the ways to refer to being baptized in water. Depending on the church or denomination you are most familiar with, being baptized in water can mean different things to different people. In some churches, babies are baptized shortly after they are born. In other churches, people are not baptized until they reach the age when they can make the choice on their own to be baptized.

We are not going to provide a theological analysis or assessment on baptism. We will simply say that we believe baptism symbolizes becoming one with Jesus in His death on the cross, being cleansed of our sins, and being raised with Him to have new life. (See **Romans 6:3-11**). We also believe in baptism by immersion in water because Jesus was baptized this way and He — as with everything else in our lives - is our example. *Then Jesus came from Galilee to the Jordan to be baptized by John. But John tried to deter him, saying, "I need to be baptized by you, and do you come to me?" Jesus replied, "Let it be so now; it is proper for us to do this to fulfill all righteousness." Then John consented. As soon as Jesus was baptized, he went up out of the water. At that moment heaven was opened, and he saw the Spirit of God descending like a dove and lighting on him. And a voice from heaven said, "This is my Son, whom I love; with him I am well pleased"* (**Matthew 3:13-17** NIV).

In addition to being our example, Jesus also tells us to do so in **Matthew 28:18-20** (NIV), *Then Jesus came to them and said, "All authority in heaven and on earth has been given to me. Therefore go and make disciples of all nations, **baptizing them in the name of the Father and of the Son and of the Holy Spirit,** and teaching them to obey everything I have commanded you..."* And in **Acts 2:38** (NIV), Peter replied, *Repent and be baptized, every one of you, in the name of Jesus Christ for the forgiveness of your sins….*

If you have recently accepted Jesus into your heart as your Lord and Savior, and you have not been water baptized, prayerfully consider doing so. If you were baptized as a baby, consider making this choice for yourself to be baptized before the Lord. (See **Romans 6**). You do not have to be baptized to go to heaven. But just like the other information we've provided in this section, getting baptized can certainly help you to grow in your relationship with Jesus.

Find out about baptism services by contacting your local church. *What are you waiting for? Get up, be baptized and wash your sins away…* (**Acts 22:16** NIV).

BAPTISM OF THE HOLY SPIRIT

But you will receive power when the Holy Spirit comes upon you… (**Acts 1:8** NLT).

We believe in the Holy Spirit. We believe that He is a genius and if we invite Him, He resides inside us. We believe that He is a gentleman and will not impose His will upon us, and He is always with us whenever we need Him and call upon Him. We believe we should always yield to the Holy Spirit when prompted (in obedience and submission to God).

Consider the following scriptures:

Matthew 12:32 (NIV)
Anyone who speaks a word against the Son of Man will be forgiven, but anyone who speaks against the Holy Spirit will not be forgiven, either in this age or in the age to come.

Luke 12:12 (NIV)
For the Holy Spirit will teach you at that time what you should say.

Luke 24:49 (NLT)
And now I will send the Holy Spirit, just as my Father promised. But stay here in the city until the Holy Spirit comes and fills you with power from heaven.

John 16:13 (AMP)
But when He, the Spirit of Truth (the Truth-giving Spirit) comes, He will guide you into all the Truth (the whole, full Truth). For He will not speak His own message [on His own authority]; but He will tell whatever He hears [from the Father; He will give the message that has been given to Him], and He will announce and declare to you the things that are to come [that will happen in the future].

John 14:16, 17 (NLT)
And I will ask the Father, and he will give you another Advocate, who will never leave you. He is the Holy Spirit, who leads into all truth. The world cannot receive him, because it isn't looking for him and doesn't recognize him. But you know him,

*because he lives with you now and later will be in
you.*

Acts 1:8 (NLT)
*But you will receive power when the Holy Spirit
comes upon you….*

Acts 2:1-4 (KJV)
*And when the day of Pentecost was fully come, they
were all with one accord in one place. And suddenly
there came a sound from heaven as of a rushing
mighty wind, and it filled all the house where they
were sitting. And there appeared unto them cloven
tongues like as of fire, and it sat upon each of them.
And they were all filled with the Holy Ghost, and
began to speak with other tongues, as the Spirit gave
them utterance.*

Also see **Galatians 5:16-26** (NLT)

John 15:26 (NLT) says, *I will send you the
Advocate—the Spirit of truth. He will come to you
from the Father and will testify all about me.* In
chapter 16 verse 14, John continues by saying,
*He will bring me glory by telling you whatever he
receives from me.* It is to our advantage to welcome
the Holy Spirit and allow Him to work through us.

If you already have Jesus in your heart and want
to also invite the Holy Spirit to indwell you, pray,
asking to be filled with the Holy Spirit.

Suggested Prayer

Lord, Your Word says You will give us an Advocate that will never leave us and will guide us into all Truth. Lord, I pray for the Holy Spirit to come upon me and fill me. I believe at this moment as I pray that I am being filled by the presence of the Holy Spirit. I believe He has come upon me and lives inside me, in Jesus' name. Amen.

OBEDIENCE

If you fully obey the LORD your God and carefully follow all his commands...God will set you high above all the nations on earth. Blessings will come upon you and accompany you if you obey the LORD your God (**Deuteronomy 28:1-2** NIV).

Obedience is defined as "the act or practice of obeying; dutiful, with respect, in agreement or submissive compliance." Frequently, when we hear the word "obedience," we think of children being obedient to their parents or pets being obedient to their owners. People may sometimes feel the word obedience has a negative meaning — being obedient means you have to give up your independence or right to freely do what you want to do. To some extent that may be true — it may also depend on the circumstances. But in its purest form, being obedient is the truest expression of respect. When children are obedient to their parents, they are demonstrating respect and honor for their parents and trust that what is being asked of them needs to be done.

James 1:22 (NASB) says, *Prove yourselves doers of the word, and not merely hearers....* This means, we shouldn't just be a ***reader*** or a ***hearer*** of the Word, but a ***doer*** of the Word. It is not enough for us to read the Bible or hear someone teach a lesson from it. We should take that Word and apply it to our lives, being obedient to do what it says. We should read and hear what God says in His Word to us, and be in agreement with it. We should do our best to conform to it, be submissive to it and be respectful of it. *All* of it, not just some of it. Not just the things that are easy or the things we like. But all of it, including things we may not like or things that may be really hard for us to do. **Numbers 23:19** (NLT) says, *God is not a man, so He does not lie. He is not human, so he does not change his mind. Has he ever spoken and failed to act? Has he ever promised and not carried it through?* So, when He gives us direction in His Word, we should do the best we can to be obedient to follow it. *Always*. Not just when it is easy or when we have nothing else to do, but at all times, because God is not a man that He would lie — He is **true** to His Word.

Anyone can be obedient **some** of the time, but that is not what God is looking for. He is looking for people who will be obedient to the best of their ability **all** of the time. He is looking for people to make the choice to no longer live by the ways of the world, but rather to live by the ways of ***His*** Word. **Matthew 6:24** (NLT) says, *No one can serve two masters. For you will hate one and love the other; you will be devoted to one and despise the other.* We shouldn't pick and choose when we will serve God and be obedient to His Word when it is convenient for us; our goal should be 100 percent obedience. Sure, there may be times when we stumble in being obedient, we are only human. As with other areas we've covered in this booklet, this too is a matter of our heart and our love for Him. We should try our best at all times, but realize when we fail that God will forgive us, and continue to try our best because we love Him.

God is clear about obedience in the Bible. He devotes **Deuteronomy 28** to the subject. Verse 1 in the New International Version says, *If you fully obey the LORD your God and carefully follow all his commands I give you today, the LORD your God will set you high above all the nations on earth.* The next part of the text speaks of blessings that will follow if we live in obedience to God's Word. They are incredible! The remainder of the text covers the "curses for disobedience," which lets us know how serious God is about this issue.

Consider spending some time reading and meditating on **Deuteronomy 28** in order to get this Word into your heart. It is an amazing Word from God which shows us that by simply being obedient — respectfully submissive to Him and His Word — He will pour great blessings out on us. But at the same time, just as there are repercussions for children who are disobedient to their parents or adults who are disrespectful to each other or to the laws of their country, there are also repercussions when people disobey God's Word. **Galatians 6:7** (NIV) says,

Do not be deceived: God cannot be mocked. A man reaps what he sows. Meaning we should not allow ourselves to be deceived, thinking that because God is loving and forgiving, we do not need to be obedient to Him and His Word. **Deuteronomy 28:15-68** makes that very clear.

HOW ARE WE TO BE OBEDIENT?

...Lord, you are our Father. We are the clay, and you are the potter. We are formed by your hand (**Isaiah 64:8** NLT).

A good place to start with how we are to be obedient is with the Ten Commandments. God gave these commandments to Moses to give to His people. The first four commandments give us direction on how we are to treat God. The last six commandments give us direction on how we are to treat one another.

COMMANDMENTS AND
BRIEF INTERPRETATIONS

Each commandment is stated below, followed by a brief interpretation.

1. *Do not worship any other gods before Me.*
   Put God first in everything in our lives.

2. *Do not make any false idols.*
   Nothing in our lives should ever be more important than God. Not money, not fame, not any material goods, not ourselves, not another person.

3. *Do not take the name of the LORD your God in vain.*
   Don't ever curse or swear using the name of God or Jesus, ever.

4. *Remember the Sabbath day to keep it holy.*
   Going to church is important.

5. *Honor your father and your mother.*
   This means that God desires for us to honor and respect our parents. We may not always agree with them or like them; they may not have been great parents. But He still asks us to honor them. If you experienced circumstances which would make honoring either of your parents difficult, pray and ask God to heal your heart and give you His grace and love to forgive them.

6. *You shall not murder.*
    Don't kill anyone.

7. *You shall not commit adultery.*
    Do not think about, fantasize about or actually
    have sex with someone you are not married to.

8. *You shall not steal.*
    Don't take something that does not belong to
    you.

9. *Do not lie.*
    Tell the truth — always. This includes all "white
    lies" or "lies of omission."

10. *Do not covet.*
    Don't wish you had something that belongs to
    someone else.

John says in **1 John 2:3-6** (NLT), ...*We can be sure
that we know him if we obey his commandments. If
someone claims, "I know God," but doesn't obey
God's commandments, that person is a liar and is
not living in the truth. But those who obey God's
word truly show how completely they love him. That
is how we know we are living in him. Those who say
they live in God should live their lives as Jesus did.*
So, living a life of obedience, as unto the Lord, is
all about living truthfully and making right choices.
Every day we are faced with literally hundreds of
choices to make. How we live our lives is a direct
reflection of those choices. No one can make them
for us — we have to do it ourselves. We choose if

we want to obey the ninth commandment and tell the truth in every situation, under every circumstance. When we make right choices, godly choices, God will reward us according to **Deuteronomy 28**. The choice is up to you.

Our prayer for you today: *Father God, we pray that every person reading this will choose to live a life of obedience to You and Your Word. We thank You, God, that they do not have to do this in their own strength but that You give them the strength they need this day and every day to make right choices, to choose You, and to do what You tell them in Your Word to do. When they come against the influences of the world and other people around them, we pray they are not negatively influenced and persuaded to make wrong choices that will result in bad consequences. We are thankful for Your forgiveness when they stumble. We pray they will make right choices every day and that it becomes easier and easier, so obedience becomes a normal way of life for them and they can experience all of the blessings You have promised them in Your Word. In Jesus' name we pray. Amen!*

FAITH

......If you have faith…like a grain of mustard seed…nothing will be impossible to you (**Matthew 17:20** AMP).

Faith — having the confidence, trust, conviction, assurance, belief, hope or expectation something is true or exists without ever actually seeing it. Having faith is usually associated with having faith in God, having faith God exists and having faith in the life and death of Jesus. We are not going to provide a theological assessment of the history of faith or provide pages of supportive documentation as to why you should have faith in God. We simply believe in living every day of our lives by faith — faith in God and faith in Jesus. Faith in a better life than the world has to offer. Faith that everything we do makes a difference in our lives and the lives around us. Faith that the Bible is the Word of God, that we are who the Bible says we are, and that we have what the Bible says we have. We don't know any other way to live than to live by faith, for *it is better to trust in the LORD than to put confidence in man* (**Psalm 118:8** KJV).

With all of that in mind, we offer the following: The simplest definition of faith in God is ***acting*** like what the Bible says is true. Faith is an act. No, faith is NOT ***putting on*** an act, as in pretending, playing, faking or putting on a front or having false pretense. Faith ***is an act*** as in how you behave, conduct yourself, or function in a given situation. Faith is believing that the Word of God is true, and *acting like it!* **Second Corinthians 5:7** (KJV) encourages us to *walk by faith, not by sight*. Some days that may mean getting out of bed and literally taking every step by faith in God's promises and not based on what is going on in the world around us — not being moved by the condition of our finances, unemployment or health issues but knowing God is in control and trusting Him and His plan for our lives.

Having faith also means believing we can be healed of sickness or disease because that is what the Word says: *He sent His Word and healed them...*(**Psalm 107:20** NKJV). *He was wounded for our transgressions, He was bruised for our iniquities: the chastisement of our peace was upon Him; and with His stripes we are healed* (**Isaiah 53:5** KJV). Don't be moved by what you see or by how things look. Don't act depressed and gloomy in any situation, but have faith in God and His Word, and have faith God can do a miracle in any situation, acting like whatever you are believing for will come to pass. Act the way you would if what you were believing for actually happened! *Act* like the cancer is healed! *Act* like the back pain is gone. *Act* like the tumor is no longer in your body. Whatever it is you are battling, *act* like you have faith in God for it to happen.

Faith can truly be healing. There are many examples in the Bible where Jesus told people their faith healed them.

Then He said to her, *"Daughter, **your faith** has healed you..."* (**Luke 8:48** NIV).

Then He said to him, *"Rise and go; **your faith** has made you well"* (**Luke 17:19** NIV).

Jesus said to him, *"Receive your sight; **your faith** has healed you"* (**Luke 18:42** NIV).

*...Jesus said...**have faith** in God [constantly]* (**Mark 11:22** AMP).

If anyone knew about faith, it was Jesus. And we can certainly trust anything Jesus says to us in the area of faith. You might say, "Well, that is all well and good for you, but I just don't have faith in anything. I have to see it to believe it." But you do have faith. **Second Corinthians 4:13** (KJV) says you do. *We having the same spirit of faith*. We are each given a measure of faith. How each of us grows in or exercises that faith is up to us as individuals. Two people can start with the same measure of faith but can grow at completely different rates depending on the amount of time they spend with the Lord, reading the Bible, praying — exercising their faith. The Word also says in **Hebrews 11:1** (KJV) *…Faith is the substance of things hoped for, the evidence of things not seen*. Just because you cannot see something happening does not mean God is not working on your need behind the scenes. Keep believing, keep trusting, ***keep having faith!*** *For verily I say unto you, that whosoever says unto this mountain, be thou removed, and be thou cast into the sea; and shall not doubt in his heart, but shall believe that those things which he says shall come to pass; he shall have whatsoever he says he has. Therefore I say to you, whatever you desire when you pray, believe that you receive them and they shall come to pass* **Mark 11:23-24** (KJV).

Spending time in God's Word is an excellent way to grow in faith, *for faith comes by hearing, and hearing by the word of God* (**Romans 10:17** NKJV). There are many great scriptures in the Bible about faith to read and meditate on. **Hebrews 11** is a great place to start. It shows examples of men and women throughout the Word, who had great faith in God. The more time you spend in the Word, reading and learning about faith, the more your faith will grow. Our prayer is that as you learn and grow in your relationship with the Lord, you will truly experience mountain-moving faith.

HEALING

...The Sun of Righteousness shall arise with healing in His wings... **Malachi 4:2** (NKJV).

A lot of times when we hear the words "heal" or "healing" we typically tend to think of a physical healing. But healing is not just physical; it can also be emotional, mental and spiritual. Anytime we have a need for healing — whether it is physical, emotional, spiritual, or mental — we can always look to the Lord and His Word for help. God made each of us and He knows everything there is to know about us. He knows how to heal us when we are hurting. Here are a few healing scriptures:

...I am the Lord, who heals you (**Exodus 15:26** NIV).

...And the Lord will take away from you all sickness, and will afflict you with none of the terrible diseases... (**Deuteronomy 7:15** NKJV).

...He heals the brokenhearted... (**Psalm 147:3** NKJV).

...And by His stripes we are healed (**Isaiah 53:5** NKJV).

...The Sun of Righteousness shall arise with healing in His wings... (**Malachi 4:2** NKJV).

God will wipe away every tear from their eyes; there shall be no more death, nor sorrow, nor crying. There shall be no more pain... (**Revelation 21:4** NKJV).

There are so many examples of people being healed in the Bible. These are not fictitious stories or parables — these are real people who had real sicknesses or diseases that God healed in each situation.

A great multitude of people are healed in **Matthew 4:23**.

Jesus heals a leper in **Matthew 8:3**.

The centurion's servant is healed in **Matthew 8:5-13**.

A woman is healed from a fever in **Matthew 8:14-15**.

All who were sick are healed in **Matthew 8:16-17**.

A paralyzed man is healed in **Matthew 9:1-7**.

The woman with the issue of blood is healed in **Matthew 9:20-22**.

Jesus heals the blind in **Matthew 9:27-30** and **Matthew 20:34.**

Every sickness and every disease is healed in **Matthew 9:35**.

A man with a withered hand is healed in **Matthew 12:9-13**.

Many were made well in **Matthew 14:35-36** and **Matthew 15:30-31**.

An epileptic boy is healed in **Matthew 17:14-18**.

God can heal *you* everywhere you hurt. What He did for all of these people, He can do for you too, if you only believe. God is a God of restoration. He longs to see His people happy and whole. He does not inflict illness on us — that is not from God. Some people may say that an illness is a test, and God only gives you what you can handle. It may be true in some cases that God will only give you what you can handle to help you learn and grow, but it does not apply in the area of sickness and disease. God *does not* make people sick or cause people to have disease. We see in **Deuteronomy 7:15** (NKJV), that *the Lord will **take away from you all sickness**, and **will afflict you with none of the terrible diseases***. The Word does not say *and God will make you sick and afflict you with terrible diseases*. It says He will take from you **all sickness**. Every sickness. Not just some sicknesses or every sickness except the one you have. No, the Words says "all" and that means every single one, **including** whatever it is you may be battling this very moment.

God loves us and does not want to see us sad, depressed, tired, overwrought, or battling any illness of any kind. So, if you find yourself in need of healing in any area, during your prayer time ask God to heal you. **James 5:13** (NKJV) says, *Is anyone among you suffering? Let him pray.* Pray on a daily basis. Meditate on the Word, especially healing scriptures. Speak the scriptures previously mentioned out loud when you pray. If you need a reminder of what God has already done for others in the area of healing, go back and review the previously mentioned scriptures that talk about all the people who were healed by God. Have faith in God — what He has done for others, He can also do for you.

Consider the following declaration (for yourself if necessary or to pray over someone else):

I am the healed of the Lord. He sent His Word to heal me and by His stripes I am healed! He is the glory and the lifter of my head and the joy and rejoicing of my soul. He is more than enough to put me over this day and every day. He is the great I Am, not the great I was or the great I will be. He is exactly what I need at this very moment. He has made me the head and not the tail, above and not beneath. God is the great Physician — He is the Lord my Healer. God will wipe away every tear from my eyes. I will no longer be in pain. The victory is mine in Jesus' name! Amen!

ETERNITY

And I give them eternal life, and they shall never lose it or perish throughout the ages (**John 10:28** AMP).

Eternity is defined as "infinite time; duration without beginning or end." It is often referred to as time without end, infinity, forever, or never-ending. With respect to God, some people may not believe in life after death or spending eternity in heaven or hell. We are not going to debate whether or not eternity is real, or provide a theological assessment of the existence of heaven and hell. We simply believe in eternity. *He has planted eternity in the human heart...*(**Ecclesiastes 3:11** NLT).

We believe there is a heaven and a hell.

[The Account of Creation] In the beginning God created the heavens... (**Genesis 1:1** NLT).

...The Lord made the heavens! (**Psalm 96:5** NLT).

...The highway to hell is broad, and its gate is wide for the many who choose that way (**Matthew 7:13** NLT).

...God did not spare even the angels who sinned. He threw them into hell, in gloomy pits of darkness, where they are being held until the day of judgment (**2 Peter 2:4** NLT).

We believe after we no longer have life in our mortal bodies, our glorified bodies will spend the rest of time with the Lord in heaven.

...[I am living in the eternity of the eternities]. I died, but see, I am alive forevermore... (**Revelation 1:18** AMP).

We believe that every choice we make on earth affects how we will spend eternity.

Here's the lesson: Use your worldly resources to benefit others and make friends. Then, when your earthly possessions are gone, they will welcome you to an eternal home (**Luke 16:9** NLT).

So whether we are here in this body or away from this body, our goal is to please him. For we must all stand before Christ to be judged. We will each receive whatever we deserve for the good or evil we have done in this earthly body. Because we understand our fearful responsibility to the Lord, we work hard to persuade others. God knows we are sincere... (**2 Corinthians 5:9-11** NLT).

BEING A CHRISTIAN — LIVING FOR JESUS

Let your light shine before men in such a way that they may see your good works, and glorify your Father who is in heaven (**Matthew 5:16** NIV).

It is challenging to be a Christian and be in the world but not of it, taking a stand for Jesus, living our lives for Jesus. Some of those challenges include temptations, frustrations, doubt, and aggravations. The Word even says in **2 Timothy 3:1-5** (NIV) ...*But mark this: There will be terrible times in the last days. People will be lovers of themselves, lovers of money, boastful, proud, abusive, disobedient to their parents, ungrateful, unholy, without love, unforgiving, slanderous, without self-control, brutal, not lovers of the good, treacherous, rash, conceited, lovers of pleasure rather than lovers of God — having a form of godliness but denying its power. Have nothing to do with them.*

We need to be ever mindful to keep our hearts and eyes on God and not on the events of the world. We need to renew ourselves daily and commit our lives to the Lord, exchanging our weakness for His strength. We need to try our best to live our lives for Jesus, letting our light shine for Him. *Let your light shine before men in such a way that they may see your good works, and glorify your Father who is in heaven* (**Matthew 5:16** NIV).

As born-again believers in Jesus Christ, how we live our daily lives is our best example to others of the love of Jesus in our hearts — the choices we make, the words we use, and how we treat others. So live your life as best you can, the way Jesus lived. Consider the following scriptures.

Isaiah 60:1 (NLT)
...Let your light shine for all to see....

Luke 6:35 (NLT)
*Love your enemies! Do good to them. Lend to them
without expecting to be repaid. Then your reward
from heaven will be very great….*

Hebrews 6:10 (NLT)
*For God is not unjust. He will not forget how hard
you have worked for him and how you have shown
your love to him by caring for other believers, as you
still do.*

1 Peter 3:14 (NLT)
*But even if you suffer for doing what is right, God
will reward you for it….*

Proverbs 25:21-22 (NLT)
*If your enemies are hungry, give them food to eat. If
they are thirsty, give them water to drink.*

1 John 4:17 (NLT)
*And as we live in God, our love grows more perfect.
So we will not be afraid on the day of judgment, but
we can face him with confidence because we live like
Jesus here in this world.*

STAYING ROOTED

*May Christ through your faith [actually] dwell (settle
down, abide, make His permanent home) in your
hearts!* (**Ephesians 3:17** AMP).

This section is about staying rooted and grounded in God...staying on course and staying focused. Not deviating or drifting away, but staying strong and developing and continuing to grow in the Lord.

If you've made the journey from the very beginning of the Grow section and read through all the information provided, you have come a long way! Congratulations! You are surely on your way to growing in your relationship with the Lord. Exactly how much you've grown and will continue to mature in the Lord will be up to you. It will be different for every person because each one of us is different, and so too are our relationships with the Lord. But one thing we all have in common is if we keep loving the Lord and spending time with Him, we will *always* continue to grow. *...Stay with and in the faith [in Christ], well-grounded and settled and steadfast, not shifting or moving away from the hope...* **Colossians 1:23** (AMP).

Remember, this is not a one-day transformation, but a complete change in who you are and how you live your life. This is a long-term relationship that will continue to grow and develop over time. **1 John 2:27** (AMP) says, *But as for you, the anointing (the sacred appointment, the unction) which you received from Him abides [permanently] in you; [so] then you have no need that anyone should instruct you. But just as His anointing teaches you concerning everything and is true and is no falsehood, so you must abide in (live in, never depart from) Him [being rooted in Him, knit to Him], just as [His anointing] has taught you [to* *do]*. Reaffirm your commitment to the Lord *every day*. Continue to spend time in the Word daily, going to church weekly, and listening to praise and worship music and God-inspired teachings. Stay close to the Lord. Keep Him, and His Word, close to you always.

Consider the following scriptures:

And I am praying that you will put into action the generosity that comes from your faith as you understand and experience all the good things we have in Christ (**Philemon 1:6** NLT).

May Christ through your faith [actually] dwell (settle down, abide, make His permanent home) in your hearts! May you be rooted deep in love and founded securely on love (**Ephesians 3:17** AMP).

So get rid of all uncleanness and the rampant outgrowth of wickedness, and in a humble (gentle, modest) spirit receive and welcome the Word which implanted and rooted [in your hearts] contains the power to save your souls (**James 1:21** AMP).

Withstand him; be firm in faith [against his onset—rooted, established, strong, immovable, and determined], knowing that the same (identical) sufferings are appointed to your brotherhood (the whole body of Christians) throughout the world (**1 Peter 5:9** AMP).

SHARE — MISSION POSSIBLE

Go ye into all the world and preach the gospel to every creature (**Mark 16:15** KJV).

Do you want to have a lasting impact on the world? Do you really want to make a difference in the lives of people around you? Do you want to be a part of the "Great Commission" and share the message of Christ with the world? *Therefore go and make disciples of all nations, baptizing them in the name of the Father and of the Son and of the Holy Spirit* (**Matthew 28:19** NIV). Do you have a passion to do something really great for God? If so, then you are in the right place.

Truly the greatest influence you can have on another person's life is to lead them to Jesus by sharing with them the life-changing message of salvation. If that is something that appeals to you, and we pray that it does, then we invite you to read through and pray about the information in this section about becoming a Messenger for Jesus and sharing the message of salvation with those who will hear it. If we all join together, we can make a great difference for Jesus. It is a mission that is *very* possible to achieve.

BECOMING A MESSENGER

*How then shall they call on Him in whom they have
not believed? And how shall they believe in Him of
whom they have not heard?* (**Romans 10:14** NKJ).

All born-again believers are called to take the Gospel
into all the world. If you have accepted Jesus Christ
as your Lord and Savior, then that means you too.
It is what we are all called to do. **Proverbs 11:30** in
The Amplified Bible says, *He who is wise captures
human lives [for God, as a fisher of men – he who
gathers and receives them for eternity]*. The Bible
has numerous references about being a messenger or
becoming a messenger for Jesus.[4]

What does it mean to be a messenger? The *American
Heritage Dictionary* defines *messenger* as "one that
carries messages or performs errands; a bearer of
news; a forerunner; a harbinger; a prophet."

Becoming a messenger for the Lord is fairly easy.
There is no formula or steps to follow or classes
to take or diploma to earn. It does not matter how
old you are, how much money you make, or your
education level. It is a matter of your heart being in
the right place. All you need is a heart for the Lord,
a desire to share all of the wonderful things Jesus
has done for you with other people — to share the
message of salvation you treasure so dearly with
others in your "sphere of influence."

Sphere of influence? Yes. No matter who we are or where we are in our lives, each of us has people in our lives we come into contact with on a regular basis. They may be friends, family members, coworkers, neighbors, social club members, hair dressers, sales clerks, telemarketers and so on. Almost every day we come into contact with someone for some reason. These are lives we can touch with the message of Jesus. Every time we come into contact with someone, it is an opportunity to show and share with them the love of Jesus.

Does that mean that every time you see someone in your sphere of influence you need to share the Gospel message with them? No, not necessarily. Trust the Lord to guide you in this area. It may be you show the life you have in Christ through the words you choose to say or those you don't say, through the things you do for others or through the things you no longer do to others. Let your life for Jesus shine through your kindness and the way you treat those around you. Your actions, in many cases, may speak louder than your words. The Lord will let you know when the time is right to share more. Or it may be you simply share what the Lord has done in your life and what He means to you. You can share how He has changed you and turned your life around — how He has healed you or made your life whole. Whatever it is that He has done for you, share it with those in your sphere of influence; let them know He can do the same for them too, if they only believe.

Go ye into all the world and preach the gospel to every creature (**Mark 16:15** KJV). Many times when we hear the scripture to take the Gospel into "all the world" and "teach the nations" we somehow think that means we have to move to another country. Scripture does not say, *taketh ye family and move to another land to share the Gospel*. It simply says "into all the world." You are part of all the world. Your family is part of all the world, as are your coworkers, friends, neighbors, etc. We don't need to move our families overseas or go on a missions trip to be in the "mission field." Our mission field can be right where we are. Everyone needs Jesus right where they are. You can reach out to unsaved members of your family or the neighbor next door. These may be the very people God is calling you to become a messenger to; they may be your mission field. Simply be open to where God is calling you to share the message of salvation.

You may be thinking, *But I am not a pastor — I don't know how to preach!* You don't need to be a pastor with a big church or the leader of a large ministry to be a messenger. Scripture does not say only people like Billy Graham or Oral Roberts are qualified to go into all the world and preach the Gospel. It says "go ye." Ye is anyone, even you! As a believer you already are a representative of the Most High God. Your words and actions are a direct reflection of who you are in Christ. You don't need to stand in a pulpit to share the message of Christ. You can do it every day of your life right where you are by showing the love of God to people in your sphere of influence.

You may be the only way some of these people come to hear or know about Jesus.

If you are considering becoming a messenger for the Lord, spend some time with Him in prayer. Talk with Him about sharing His Word with "every creature." Ask Him to show you what He would have you do. Be still and listen to what He has to say to you.

MESSENGER DECLARATION

What now? Are you ready to become a messenger for Jesus, sharing the Gospel message with those in your sphere of influence? If you're not sure, keep praying. Listen to the Lord; He will guide you, and you will know when you are ready.

If you are ready now, then we invite you to speak the following declarations out loud to the Lord. (No, you do not have to speak these words out loud to be able to share the message of salvation with others. We simply offer them as a way for you to express your commitment).

- Lord, I declare to You this day that I want to become a messenger for You, sharing the message of salvation with those in my personal sphere of influence and anyone else You put on my heart.

- God, I truly believe the greatest influence I can have in another person's life is to lead them to Jesus.

- God, I offer myself to You. Use me as a vessel to carry the message of salvation to others.

- God, I declare that I will have a spirit of boldness and not a spirit fear or intimidation when presented with an opportunity to share Your message.

- I declare I will take this responsibility seriously.

- Lord, I confess I will spend time with You daily and in Your Word to strengthen my spirit and hear what You would have me do for You.

- I declare that I will live honorably before You, Lord, in both my public and personal life so I am spotless and free of any accusations. I want what I say to be directly supported by what I do — how I behave. I will not do one thing and say another or speak out of both sides of my mouth.

- I will act kindly toward everyone I come into contact with. I will not be rude or disrespectful but I will walk in the love of Christ.

- I will dress professionally and modestly, not sloppily or provocatively, as I am a representative of Jesus Christ.

- I confess I will simply share the message of salvation, the Word of God. I will not enter into debates with others or try to impose my own will or opinions upon others.

- I confess I will not judge anyone as not being worthy of receiving Jesus.

- I declare to You this day, Lord, that I will commit my time, talents, and treasures to doing my part in taking Your message into all the world.

- I declare that I will be obedient to You in this area, Lord, however and wherever You lead me.

- I declare I am Your missionary, Lord.

- I declare I am a messenger for You, Lord, and I am dedicated to Your service.

- I make these declarations in Jesus' name. Amen!

God bless you! You have just made an incredible commitment to the Lord. Continue to pray and prepare your heart. Always know God will be right there with you each and every time you have the opportunity to share His Word. As the Lord gives you opportunities to be a messenger, keep in mind the words of **John 13:16** (NIV)...*I tell you the truth, no servant is greater than his master, nor is a **messenger** greater than the one who sent him.*

BEING A MESSENGER

Consider the following prayer as you embark on your new journey.

*God, I believe You have called me to become a messenger for You. I want my life to make a difference for You, God. I know this life is not about me and what I want, but it is about You, giving my heart to You and serving You in every way I can. God, show me what You would have me do for You. Lord, You tell us in **Mark 16:15** (KJV) to "go ye into all the world, and preach the gospel to every creature." God, if it is important enough for You to say it, then that is what I want to do for You. Equip me, Lord. Give me a spirit of boldness to approach the people You put on my heart to share the message of salvation. In Jesus' name I pray. Amen!*

Make a list of people or groups of people in your sphere of influence who do not know Jesus as their personal Savior. Consider saying the following prayer for these people daily and listen to what the Lord would have you do for them. It may be He wants you to share the message of salvation with them or to pray for them on a daily basis. Or you may simply show them the love of Christ through your actions when you are around them. Be obedient to whatever God puts on your heart in this area.

Salvation Prayer for People in Your Sphere of Influence

I thank You, Lord, first and foremost for my salvation. I am truly blessed that I am saved. God, I lift up [name, group of names] to You, Lord. I pray for their salvation. God, I pray that You soften their hearts and open their eyes and their ears to You. God, I pray that You place people in their lives who will share the Gospel message with them. I pray that if I am to be one of those people to share Your message with them that You show me when and how to do it. I thank You in advance for giving me the words to speak to them. I thank You in advance for providing the perfect timing to share Your message. I thank You, Lord, that they will be receptive to hear what You would have me say to them and that You are preparing their hearts right now in Jesus' name. Lord, I thank You for the work You are doing in [name, group of names] life (lives). I thank You, Lord, that You hold [him, her, them], in the palm of Your hand. In Jesus' name I pray. Amen!

WHAT NEXT?

Continue to pray and keep living a life for Christ. How you live your life on a daily basis — what you say, how you act, the choices you make, how you treat others — can be the greatest way you show your love for Christ to others.

When God gives you a chance to share the Gospel with someone, keep in mind the declarations you've already made. In fact, feel free to speak these out loud on a daily basis as part of your prayer time as a reminder of the commitments you made to the Lord to be His messenger. They will strengthen and encourage you.

Remember, God is always right there with you, helping you with every word, thought and action. Be humble and not judgmental — we've all sinned and God desires that we all be saved. Most of all, remember it is all about Him, and not about us. We believe you will do great things for the Lord! You are *forever changed!* May God richly bless you.

ENDNOTES

[1] **1 Corinthians 13:1-8**

1 If I [can] speak in the tongues of men and [even] of angels, but have not love (that reasoning, intentional, spiritual devotion such as is inspired by God's love for and in us), I am only a noisy gong or a clanging cymbal.

2 And if I have prophetic powers (the gift of interpreting the divine will and purpose), and understand all the secret truths and mysteries and possess all knowledge, and if I have [sufficient] faith so that I can remove mountains, but have not love (God's love in me) I am nothing (a useless nobody).

3 Even if I dole out all that I have [to the poor in providing] food, and if I surrender my body to be burned or in order that I may glory, but have not love (God's love in me), I gain nothing.

4 I endure long and I am patient and kind; I am never envious nor boil over with jealousy, I am not boastful or vainglorious, I do not display myself haughtily.

5 I am not conceited (I am not arrogant and I am not inflated with pride); I am not rude (unmannerly) I do not act unbecomingly. I do not insist on my own rights or my own ways, for I am not self-seeking; I am not touchy I am not fretful, I am not resentful; I take no account of the evil done to me [I pay no attention to a suffered wrong].

6 I do not rejoice at injustice or unrighteousness, but I rejoice when right and truth prevail.

7 I bear up under anything and everything that comes my way, I am ever ready to believe the best of every person, my hopes are fadeless under all circumstances, and I endure everything [without weakening].

8 I never fail [I never fade out I never become obsolete or come to an end].

14 For this reason [seeing the greatness of this plan by which I am built together in Christ], I bow my knees before the Father of our Lord Jesus Christ,

15 For Whom every family in heaven and on earth is named [that Father from Whom all fatherhood takes its title and derives me].

16 May He grant me out of the rich treasury of His glory to be strengthened and reinforced with mighty power in the inner man by the [Holy] Spirit [Himself indwelling my innermost being and personality].

17 May Christ through my faith [actually] dwell (settle down, abide, make His permanent home) in my heart! May I be rooted deep in love and founded securely on love,

18 That I may have the power and be strong to apprehend and grasp with all the saints [God's devoted people, the experience of that love] what is the breadth and length and height and depth [of it];

19 [That I may really come] to know [practically, through experience for myself] the love of Christ, which far surpasses mere knowledge [without experience]; that I may be filled [through all my being] unto all the fullness of God [that I may have the richest measure of the divine Presence, and myself become a body wholly filled and flooded with God Himself]!

20 Now to Him Who, by (in consequence of) the [action of His] power that is at work within me, is able to [carry out His purpose and] do superabundantly, far over and above all that I [dare] ask or think [infinitely beyond my highest prayers, desires, thoughts, hopes, or dreams].

[3] **Colossians 1:9-14**

9 For this reason I also, from the day I heard of it, have not ceased to pray and make [special] request for myself, [asking] that I may be filled with the full (deep and clear) knowledge of His will in all spiritual wisdom [in comprehensive insight into the ways and purposes of God] and in understanding and discernment of spiritual things—

10 That I may walk (live and conduct myself) in a manner worthy of the Lord, fully pleasing to Him and desiring to please Him in all things, bearing fruit in every good work and steadily growing and increasing in and by the knowledge of God [with fuller, deeper, and clearer insight, acquaintance, and recognition].

11 [I pray] that I may be invigorated and strengthened with all power according to the might of His glory, [to exercise] every kind of endurance and patience (perseverance and forbearance) with joy,

12 Giving thanks to the Father, Who has qualified and made me fit to share the portion which is the inheritance of the saints (God's holy people) in the Light.

13 [The Father] has delivered and drawn me to Himself out of the control and the dominion of darkness and has transferred me into the kingdom of the Son of His love,

14 In Whom I have my redemption through His blood, [which means] the forgiveness of my sins.

Scriptures for becoming a messenger
(all scripture references are from The Amplified Bible).

Genesis 50:16 (AMP)
And they sent a **messenger** to Joseph, saying, Your
father commanded before he died…

Judges 5:23 (AMP)
Curse Meroz, said the **messenger** of the Lord. Curse
bitterly its inhabitants, because they came not to the
help of the Lord, to the help of the Lord against the
mighty!

1 Samuel 4:17
The **messenger** replied, Israel fled before the
Philistines, and there has been a great slaughter
among the people. Also your two sons, Hophni and
Phinehas, are dead, and the ark of God is captured.

1 Samuel 23:27
But a **messenger** came to Saul, saying, Make haste
and come, for the Philistines have made a raid on the
land.

2 Samuel 11:19
And he charged the **messenger**, When you have
finished reporting matters of the war to the king,

2 Samuel 11:22
So the **messenger** went and told David all for which
Joab had sent him.

2 Samuel 11:23
The **messenger** said to David, Surely the men
prevailed against us and came out to us in to the field,
but we were upon them even to the entrance of the
gate.

2 Samuel 11:25
Then David said to the **messenger**, Say to Joab, Let not this thing disturb you, for the sword devours one as well as another. Strengthen your attack upon the city and overthrow it. And encourage Joab.

2 Samuel 15:13
And there came a **messenger** to David, saying, The hearts of the men of Israel have gone after Absalom.

1 Kings 19:2
Then Jezebel sent a **messenger** to Elijah, saying, So let the gods do to me, and more also, if I make not your life as the life of one of them by this time tomorrow.

1 Kings 22:13
The **messenger** who went to call Micaiah said to him, Behold now, the prophets unanimously declare good to the king. Let your answer, I pray you, be like theirs, and say what is good.

2 Kings 5:10
Elisha sent a **messenger** to him, saying, Go and wash in the Jordan seven times, and your flesh shall be restored and you shall be clean.

2 Kings 6:32
Now Elisha sat in his house, and the elders sat with him. And the king sent a man from before him [to behead Elisha]. But before the **messenger** arrived, Elisha said to the elders, See how this son of [Jezebel] a murderer is sending to remove my head? Look, when the **messenger** comes, shut the door and hold it fast against him. Is not the sound of his master's feet [just] behind him?

2 Kings 6:33
And while Elisha was talking with them, behold, [the **messenger**] came to him [and then the king came also]. And [the relenting king] said, This evil is from the Lord! Why should I any longer wait [expecting Him to withdraw His punishment? What, Elisha, can be done now]?

2 Kings 9:18
So one on horseback went to meet him and said, Thus says the king: Is it peace? And Jehu said, What have you to do with peace? Rein in behind me. And the watchman reported, The **messenger** came to them, but he does not return.

2 Kings 10:8
When a **messenger** came and told him, They have brought the heads of the king's sons, he said, Lay them in two heaps at the entrance of the city gate until morning.

2 Chronicles 18:12
The **messenger** who went to call Micaiah said to him, Behold, the words of the prophets foretell good to the king with one accord. So let your word be like one of them, and speak favorably.

Job 1:14
And there came a **messenger** to Job and said, The oxen were plowing and the donkeys feeding beside them,

Job 33:23
[God's voice may be heard] if there is for the hearer a **messenger** or an angel, an interpreter, one among a thousand, to show to man what is right for him [how to be upright and in right standing with God],

Proverbs 13:17
A wicked **messenger** falls into evil, but a faithful ambassador brings healing.

Proverbs 17:11
An evil man seeks only rebellion; therefore a stern and pitiless **messenger** shall be sent against him.

Proverbs 25:13
Like the cold of snow [brought from the mountains] in the time of harvest, so is a faithful **messenger** to those who send him; for he refreshes the life of his masters.

Ecclesiastes 5:6
Do not allow your mouth to cause your body to sin, and do not say before the **messenger** [the priest] that it was an error or mistake. Why should God be [made] angry at your voice and destroy the work of your hands?

Isaiah 42:19
Who is blind but My servant [Israel]? Or deaf like My **messenger** whom I send? Who is blind like the one who is at peace with Me [who has been admitted to covenant relationship with Me]? Yes, who is blind like the Lord's servant?

Jeremiah 49:14
I have heard a report from the Lord, and a **messenger** is sent to the nations, saying, Gather together and come against her! And rise up for the battle.

Jeremiah 51:31
One post shall run to meet another and one
messenger to meet another to show the king of
Babylon that his city is taken on every side and to its
farthest end,

Ezekiel 23:40
And furthermore, you have sent for men to come from
afar, to whom a **messenger** was sent; and behold,
they came—those for whom you washed yourself,
painted your eyelids, and decked yourself with
ornaments;

Haggai 1:13
Then Haggai, the Lord's **messenger**, spoke the
Lord's message to the people saying, I am with you,
says the Lord.

Zechariah 2:8
For thus said the Lord of hosts, after [His] glory
had sent me [His **messenger**] to the nations who
plundered you—for he who touches you touches the
apple or pupil of His eye:

Zechariah 2:9
Behold, I will swing my hand over them and they shall
become plunder for those who served them. Then you
shall know (recognize and understand) that the Lord
of hosts has sent me [His **messenger**].

Zechariah 2:11
And many nations shall join themselves to the Lord
in that day and shall be My people. And I will dwell in
the midst of you, and you shall know (recognize and
understand) that the Lord of hosts has sent me [His
messenger] to you.

One Man One Message
P.O. Box 8513
St. Louis, Missouri 63126
onemanonemessage.org